Original title:
Under the Tidal Moonlight

Copyright © 2025 Creative Arts Management OÜ
All rights reserved.

Author: Derek Caldwell
ISBN HARDBACK: 978-1-80587-428-7
ISBN PAPERBACK: 978-1-80587-898-8

Luminous Whispers of the Deep Sea

Fish wear wigs and dance around,
While octopuses twirl—so profound.
Seashells gossip, telling tales,
Of squids in suits and jelly sails.

A crab recites a comic tale,
While turtles sip their algae ale.
Starfish clap with glee and cheer,
As sea cucumbers lose their fear.

Starlit Visions on the Ocean's Canvas

A dolphin rides a wave on cue,
Singing songs of the ocean blue.
Seagulls jest, they steal a fry,
As a seal rolls by, oh my!

Bubbles pop like joyous tunes,
While clownfish wear their funny balloons.
The night is filled with laughter bright,
In this wacky sea's delight.

Tides that Hold the Night's Secrets

Anemones tickle the passing fish,
While turtles make a secret wish.
Crabs in shoes take a dazzling stroll,
They turn the tide—oh, what a goal!

Whales splash paint like artists true,
As plankton dance in neon hue.
Their midnight fun a sight divine,
In the ocean's jesting line.

The Gentle Pull of Lunar Waves

A mermaid plays the piano grand,
Shells are scattered, a jazzy band.
Whispers ride on swaying kelp,
As fish high five themselves in yelp.

Moonbeams glint on fishy hats,
With dolphins cracking silly chats.
The tides tease secrets, laugh and sway,
In this silly, fishy play.

Night's Caress on Waters So Deep

The fish are dancing, quite a sight,
They hold a party, all through the night.
With bubbles popping, laughter erupts,
Even sea turtles are doing hiccups.

Stars laugh along, with a wink and a glow,
Seagulls are swooping, putting on a show.
They steal a crab's snack, oh what a prank,
And under the waves, the jellyfish drank.

A dolphin decides to wear a hat,
Splashed with colors, a sight to chat.
They surf on the waves with laughter so grand,
While a clam tells jokes, his best in the sand.

The night holds secrets in its embrace,
As fish strut around, each with a face.
So join the fun in a splashy spree,
Where the water's alive, come swim with me!

Ocean Secrets Illuminated by the Skies

A crab in a tux, just feeling so fine,
He said to a snail, 'You'll rush for the wine!'
They toast to the tides with seaweed snacks,
While the fish join in, shaking their backs.

The waves giggle softly, tickling the shore,
Shells are applauding, they just want more.
The octopus juggles, a marvelous feat,
While sand dollars dance on their tiny feet.

A whale sings loudly, hits every note,
The starfish dance wildly, they're on a boat.
A flatfish plays guitar with a shell,
In this ocean bazaar, all is well!

The moon shines bright, in its disco ball dress,
As the sea creatures groove, the water's a mess.
With laughter and jokes, they party all night,
In this watery world, everything feels right!

Luminous Echoes at the Water's Edge

The clams are gossiping, chatting with glee,
'Have you heard about Gary? He's stuck in a tree!'
They titter and chuckle, oh what a jest,
While bubbles float up, inviting the rest.

A seahorse painted in polka dot style,
Is plucking a tune, it's been a while.
He strums on a coral, such rhythm and flare,
The anemones sway, caught up in the air.

'Why did the fish cross the deep, dark sea?'
It quipped to a crab, 'To avoid a big bee!'
And laughter erupts in waves across sand,
As the moonlight twinkles, a sparkle so grand.

The tide comes in, the fun won't stop,
As starry-eyed otters perform a flip flop.
With echoes of joy under starlit delight,
In this marvelous world, we party each night!

Serene Whispers of the Abyss

In the deep, fish wear hats,
Making plans with the chatting crabs.
They joke about the sea's cool breeze,
And dance like they've just won jabs.

A squid shows off its lovely ink,
Throwing parties just for the shad.
While jellyfish twirl like they boast,
The starfish joins in, feeling rad.

Eels play leapfrog with the waves,
Their slippery moves are quite a laugh.
A clam shares secrets with a shrimp,
As dolphins offer to do the math.

With bubbles bursting from their glee,
The ocean sings its funny tune.
In this realm of playful tides,
Life's a joke beneath the moon.

Celestial Orchestrations of the Sea

Seagulls sing their off-key song,
While barnacles watch from the rocks.
Shells are keeping a rhythm tight,
Crabs snap their claws as if in clocks.

A whale sways to the ocean's beat,
Performing dances, bold and wide.
"Is that a kraken?" echoes loud,
But it's just a squid, on a joyride.

The shoals parade in wild display,
Fins flutter like a flag in wind.
With fishy humor all around,
Every scale with laughter grinned.

Coral reefs throw upbeat fests,
Bubbles bubbling with delight.
Under waves, the fun persists,
With ocean's laughter, pure and bright.

Dreams Rising on Midnight Tides

At midnight, dreams begin to float,
Seashells giggle, slapping each other.
A crab recites a bedtime tale,
While the octopus plays the mother.

The starlight winks, a playful tease,
As fish swim by on noodle legs.
Their antics stir the sandy floor,
With shrimps pulling pranks as they beg.

A dolphin leaps, then slips on slime,
Creating ripples of joyful air.
The seaweed's swaying to the tune,
Of laughter echoing everywhere.

In this watery world of dreams,
A party brews beneath the tide.
With every wave a chuckle breaks,
As cute sea critters slip and glide.

The Rhythm of Driftwood and Dreams

Driftwood dances on the shore,
With barnacles joining in the beat.
A log rolls over a stunned old crab,
Who claims it's now a dancing seat.

Seashells form a conga line,
Shaking their shades in vibrant cheer.
A fish in sunglasses leads the charge,
While clowns of the sea draw near.

The tide breaks jokes as it rolls back,
Splashing laughter on sandy ground.
Even the sun starts to giggle,
With seaside antics all around.

In this fiesta of the sea,
Every wave whispers funny dreams.
With driftwood clapping along the shore,
Ocean's joy bursts at the seams.

Sentinels of the Midnight Tide

The crabs all dance with glee,
Shuffling sideways, can't you see?
They wear tiny hats made of shells,
While singing songs of the ocean swells.

A starfish tried to toe-tap too,
But ended up stuck in some goo.
With a wink, the jellyfish swayed,
Laughing at all the mess they made.

Seagulls squawked, a raucous choir,
One landed on a lifeguard's tire.
The beach ball bounced right into a wave,
"Catch me if you can!" it gave.

The tide giggled as it rolled back in,
With each little splash, the fun would begin.
A clam snapped shut, a tiny laugh,
In this midnight mischief by the staff.

Reflections of a Starry Cascade

Bubbles drift like dreams afloat,
A fish in a bowtie on a boat.
He took one leap, and off he went,
Right into a kid's ice cream tent!

Stars above twinkled with delight,
As the octopus danced in the moonlight.
With eight silly limbs, he did a spin,
While everyone laughed until they grinned.

A sea turtle wearing sunglasses cool,
Cruised by a group of dolphins in school.
They played tag, oh what a sight,
Under laughter's echo, pure delight.

The tide rolled in, with a giant splash,
"Don't get wet!" they all did dash.
Yet one brave seagull took a dive,
"I'm just practicing to stay alive!"

The Night's Embrace on Sandy Shores

The beach is buzzing with whacky sights,
Waves tickle toes, oh what a fright!
A crab hitches a ride on a flip-flop,
Heading to a party nonstop!

With sunscreen dripping, a kid applies,
He slipped and fell, oh that's no surprise!
His friends all giggled, rolling around,
A sandy disaster was what they found.

The moon grinned down, casting its glow,
As squirrels built castles, putting on a show.
They found a beach ball, tossed it high,
"Watch out!" they chirped, "It's gonna fly!"

In the chaos of laughter, the night took flight,
As waves applauded, all was just right.
With a splash and a cheer, the fun did unfold,
Under stars of laughter, legends retold.

Beneath the Glowing Celestial Veil

A dolphin wore a flower crown,
Chasing surfboards all around town.
With a flip and a twist, it sparkled bright,
A beach party buzzed well into the night.

Kites flew high, tangled in trees,
As seagulls plotted a snack with ease.
They snatched chips from an unsuspecting hand,
While the kids just laughed, "What a plan!"

An old pirate, with a parrot so loud,
Declared he'd find treasure beneath the crowd.
But all that he found was a lost flip-flop,
And a crab that danced and wouldn't stop.

As waves crashed down, they cheered with glee,
"Who needs treasure? We found a sea spree!"
With laughter echoing, the tide bowed low,
Under the night glow, they stole the show.

When the Stars Kiss the Ocean

The fish wear crowns made of stars,
They giggle as they swim near bars.
Crabs in tuxedos dance on sand,
While jellyfish star in a rock band.

Seagulls dive, trying to impress,
With flips and tricks in their own dress.
A clam cracks jokes, makes everyone cheer,
While dolphins toast with seashell beer.

Starfish play dice on a floating raft,
Hoping for luck in the ocean's craft.
Octopuses juggle colorful pebbles,
While sea cucumbers form their fables.

Bubbles rise like balloons in flight,
As waves break into laughter at night.
With every splash, the fun unfolds,
Beneath the twinkles, stories are told.

Mystical Reflections of the Deep

A mermaid lost her favorite shoe,
Asked a shark if he'd seen it too.
They laughed so hard, they made a splash,
Setting off a wave that caused a crash.

Clownfish joke with a serious look,
"Why didn't the crab read the book?"
Coral giggles in shades of pink,
As blowfish puff up, spill jokes with a wink.

Starry-eyed turtles race in glee,
While seaweed waltzes in harmony.
An octopus tries out slapstick tricks,
As fish make fun of his crazy kicks.

From bubbles brew laughter and cheer,
As creatures gather, far and near.
In depths where the playful sway and leap,
Funny tales dwell in the secrets they keep.

Enchanted Shores at Dusk

Crabs scamper quick in a last-minute dash,
While seagulls complain, feeling quite brash.
Sandcastles crumble as laughter rains,
With seashells chuckling at their pains.

The tide rolls in with a teasing embrace,
Surfers enjoy a slippery race.
A mermaid grins, tail all aglow,
While sea turtles burst into a show.

Seashells whisper secrets of the day,
As the wind joins in, blowing jokes their way.
Stars peek out, can't help but chuckle,
While sand dunes sway with a playful shuffle.

As night paints the scene in silvery hues,
The ocean's song sings amusing tunes.
In this realm where silliness flows,
Friends gather 'round for laughter that grows.

The Melodies of Distant Shores

A whale's tune turns into a rap,
As dolphins jump and don a cap.
Seashells join with a raucous cheer,
Echoing giggles for all to hear.

Anemones sway to the upbeat sound,
With all the fish dancing, round and round.
The sand knows all the best dad jokes,
Making sure the ocean never chokes.

Seagulls caw in a comical way,
Trying to steal a fry from a ray.
Starfish strum on a coral guitar,
While crabs play bingo from afar.

As waves crash in, laughter breaks free,
Creating rhythms of pure glee.
In the harmony of night's embrace,
Funny melodies find their place.

Nightfall's Embrace on Shimmering Waters

The crabs hold a dance, quite absurd,
While seagulls sing songs that are blurred.
A fish loudly coughs and then flops,
As the moon's glowing belly just hops.

Starfish lounge like they own the place,
While jellyfish float with quite the grace.
On sandy shores, laughter rings out,
As mermaids join in without a doubt.

The waves tell tales of mishaps galore,
With seaweed wigs on the ocean floor.
A clam with a shell of wild design,
Becomes the style icon—weirdly divine.

Under the laughter of night's great jokes,
Even the dolphins crack silly hoaxes.
In this twilight world where giggles are free,
The ocean's a circus, come join in glee!

Serenading the Silence of the Sea

Octopuses juggle their dinner tonight,
Mussels sing ballads in whimsical flight.
A whale tells a joke, but it's all in the wave,
Making fish laugh till they're gasping to save.

The starry-eyed plankton twinkle and twirl,
As clownfish perform in a watery swirl.
With shells as their stage, barnacles cheer,
While crabs root on with some seaweed beer.

Seashells gossip in whispers so clear,
Of silly sea tales that everyone hears.
Anemones dance, adjusting their wigs,
While seahorses waltz, pulling off swigs.

In this grand ocean, mirth takes its reign,
Where laughter and silliness float with the grain.
Every splash holds a chuckle, a grin,
As the night hums a tune where fun can begin!

Tales Spun in the Ocean's Light

The conch shell's tales are unique and grand,
Where goofy crab races are wholly unplanned.
Seahorses giggle, tails tied in a knot,
While starfish pretend they're a friendly mascot.

Mollusks read poems of whimsical lore,
With squids painting jesters on coral's rich floor.
They hold a parade, with bubbles that burst,
As laughter and joy quench their silly thirst.

The tide tugs at seaweed with playful delight,
While blowfish puff up for a comical fright.
Cling to the laughter, let worries all sink,
The ocean's a riddle, so share a good wink!

So gather your friends by the shimmering brine,
Where undersea antics twirl into time.
A circle of joy where the moon peeks through,
With giggles and splashes, just wait 'til it's two!

Glowing Veils of the Midnight Tide

The lighthouse shivers, what's up with that beam?
Glad crabs can't see, or they'd run from the gleam.
A dolphin declares, 'I'm the king of the waves!'
Until a fish jokes, 'But you still ride your knaves!'

The seafoam giggles, tickling the shore,
As shells try to rhyme, but can't find the score.
Jellybeans pop in the midnight delight,
With squishy charms dancing, what a sight!

Under the glows of the silvery crest,
Fish throw confetti and lead the quest.
An octopus poet writes stories of fun,
While all the sea critters join in the run.

So come close, dear friend, to this magical night,
Where laughter's a treasure that shines oh-so-bright.
In glowing waves blooming, let joy be your guide,
In this funny realm, we'll forever abide!

Moonbeams and Mysterious Depths

In the night, the waves do dance,
Fish wear shades, giving romance.
Octopus in a party hat,
Jellyfish jive, how about that?

Seagulls squawk, a confused tune,
Starfish rave beneath the moon.
Crabs in sneakers, crabs in socks,
Holiday lights on ocean rocks.

Dolphins dive with winking eyes,
Finding treasure, much to surprise.
Clams tell jokes, they're quite the hit,
While seaweed dances, never quit.

Mermaids giggle, tails in a twist,
"Did you see that?"—they just can't resist.
Underwater laughs are quite absurd,
Who knew the sea was so disturbed?

A Ballet of Light on the Waves

Waves twirl in a nightly trance,
Barnacles joining in the dance.
Moonlight winks and dips its toes,
While sea turtles strike a pose.

Shells applaud with tiny hands,
Crabs are judging the dance bands.
Starfish spin in roundabouts,
While seahorses shout out shouts.

Gulls swing low in pirouette,
Joey the fish couldn't fret.
Manta rays glide, smooth and bright,
Taking selfies in the night.

Bubbles pop like winning cheers,
Underwater, joy appears.
A splash of fun, a finned parade,
In this ballet, jokes are made!

Moonlit Footprints in Soft Sand

Footprints wander on the shore,
A crab hops by, and what's in store?
Sandcastles built with cheesy style,
Seagulls eyeing them all the while.

A squawking bird gets stuck in goo,
With every stomp it slips right through.
Tide pulls back with a sneaky grin,
"Longer legs? Well, let's begin!"

Oysters laugh beneath the sand,
As puddles splash from a tiny hand.
"Look at me! A mermaid's tail!"
But it's just a fishy scale.

Shells whisper tales of evening fun,
In the twilight, they've just begun.
The shore's a stage, the sea's the band,
Laughter echoes, hand in hand.

The Tide's Gentle Lament

The tide sighs softly, waves complain,
"Where's my beach ball? It's gone again!"
Seashells gossip on the swells,
With tales of fish that cast their spells.

The moon, it chuckles, bright and bold,
"Let me tell you 'bout the tales of old!"
Fiddler crabs like tiny clowns,
Dancing round in their best gowns.

A whale sings low, a lullaby,
Fish yawn wide, as stars float by.
Octopuses twist, making art,
With each new wave, they play their part.

Laughter floats on ocean breeze,
The tide laments with joyful ease.
"Who knew my nights were such a show?
I've got the best jokes, just so you know!"

Chasing Shadows of the Night

In the dark, where shadows play,
I tripped on seaweed, yelled, "Hooray!"
The fish all laughed, they took a dive,
While I just flailed, trying to survive.

Crabs joined in, a fancy waltz,
I clumsily stepped on their salty vaults.
They clapped their claws with rhythmic beat,
And danced about my soggy feet.

Moonlight shimmered, oh so bright,
I swear I saw a fish take flight!
The stars above began to tease,
As I splashed 'round with giggling ease.

But in the end, with a grand hoorah,
I raced the waves, forgot my flaw.
In moonlit pranks, so wild and bold,
The ocean's laughter never grows old.

Secrets in Moonshadowed Waters

Beneath the waves, secrets abound,
A fish in shades of blue and brown.
He winked at me with a sly little grin,
Said, "Join the party, just dive right in!"

They host a ball with bubbles and glee,
While an octopus juggles like he's free.
The seaweed waved like a fancy gown,
And everyone laughed, never a frown.

A starfish said, "You've got two left fins!"
I spun around, but still couldn't win.
The sea urchins snickered, what a sight,
As I tried to dance in the pale moonlight.

But with a flip and a splash so grand,
I discovered joy in this watery land.
The secrets flew as we laughed and swirled,
In moonshadowed waters, my heart unfurled.

Twilight Meetings with the Ocean's Heart

At twilight's edge, the waves do play,
I met a dolphin, bright as day.
He twisted, turned with such pure flair,
While I just bobbed in jelly-like air.

He asked me, "Can you do a flip?"
I answered with a clumsy trip.
The jellyfish giggled, oh what a sight,
As I flopped and flailed in the fading light.

With shells as drums, we made a beat,
I swayed with rhythm, my wiggly feet.
The moonbeams caught our merry dance,
As crabs clapped claws, giving a chance.

Now every twilight, we meet and cheer,
For laughter reigns in the salty sphere.
In ocean's heart, we find our song,
With giggles and splashes, we all belong.

The Ocean's Soul Bathing in Light

The ocean grinned, her soul aglow,
With tidal waves that start to flow.
I splashed around, a silly sight,
Chasing waves under stars so bright.

A seagull swooped with a sparkle high,
"No diving here!" he squawked with a guy.
I laughed and said, "Just watch my flair!"
As I belly-flopped without a care.

The sea stars twinkled, sharing the joke,
As a whale swam by with a heartbeat poke.
"You're quite the splash, my silly friend!"
They cheered me on, urging to transcend.

In moon's soft laugh, we sing and play,
As the ocean's soul beams night away.
With every splash, a joyful tune,
We dance beneath a friendly moon.

Moonlit Dances of the Deep

The fish wear shoes for their big dance,
They twirl and spin in a silly prance.
Starfish clap with their tiny hands,
While seaweed sways like it understands.

Crabs break out in their funky shoes,
Belly-flopping, they sing the blues.
An octopus joins, with eight arms wide,
They all groove together, full of pride.

Jellyfish bounce with an elegant grace,
While dolphins flip in a fast-paced race.
They laugh in bubbles, with glee in their eyes,
Under this glow, the party never dies.

So come take a dive into the fun,
In the dance of the deep, everyone won.
With laughter and joy, the ocean will share,
A night of pure fun, with friends everywhere.

Secrets of the Ocean's Glow

The clams tell tales that no one believes,
Of treasure chests and purple leaves.
Sea turtles gossip while digging a hole,
About a rogue wave that tried to take control.

Crabs wear hats like the finest lore,
Debating who'll win the next underwater score.
With whispers of pearls and laughter galore,
They chant silly songs that echo the shore.

A dolphin splashes, making quite a scene,
While sardines dance like they're on a cuisine.
Octopuses juggle, with a wink and a grin,
In the glow, there's always mischief to spin.

So secrets abound in the glowing waves,
Of mischief, of laughter, like oceanic braves.
The night holds stories, we can't help but know,
In the depths of this place, where silly fish go.

Reflections in Celestial Waters

The moon's a mirror in the ocean's hair,
Reflecting clowns in a watery fair.
Seahorses prance with a comical flair,
While bubbles burst like giggles in the air.

Fish wear sunglasses, strutting along,
Finishing their dance with a catchy song.
Starfish join in with a chorus so bright,
They twinkle like stars in the cool, calm night.

The whales joke about who's the biggest fish,
While everyone laughs, making a wild wish.
Turtles join tails for an awkward show,
In reflections that shimmer, their smiles all glow.

So dive into this bizarre, moonlit dream,
Where chuckles echo and laughter will beam.
Under these stars, let your troubles just float,
In the whimsical waters, where jests lightly coat.

Lullabies of the Siren's Tide

The sirens sing with a cheeky delight,
As fish tap dance under the pale moonlight.
They croon about bubbles and warrior fish,
Who wish for a moment to grant a small wish.

In currents they giggle, weaving their tale,
About dolphins who claim they can ride a whale.
With voices so sweet and a wink of the eye,
They send silly dreams through the night sky.

In the depths where the giggling never ends,
The seahorses prance, inviting their friends.
With each little lullaby sung under the night,
They tickle the waves with pure, joyful light.

So let your heart dance with these tunes in the deep,
As the ocean's laughter helps your worries sleep.
For in this bright tide where silliness swells,
The lullabies sing all the great ocean's spells.

Moonlit Serenade of the Seafarers

Beneath the glow, a sailor's pride,
His trusty map, a fishy guide.
With nets all tangled, he starts to sing,
Fish leap around, they join his fling.

In moonlit dreams, they swap tall tales,
Of pirates, treasure, and windy gales.
A mermaid winks, makes him blush bright,
He spills his grog, a slippery sight!

The gulls fly by, with laughter loud,
A foghorn's honk brings in the crowd.
"Yo-ho-ho!" shouts the jolly crew,
While crabs do a dance, a waltz for two.

Every wave's a giggle, what a scene,
As lanterns sway, all glimmering green.
With fishy jokes and lots of cheer,
They toast to the sea, and down another beer!

Echoes of the Deepened Horizon

To the sea's edge, the sailors roam,
With seaweed hats, declaring home.
The ocean laughs, it splashes back,
As jellyfish start their dance attack.

On distant shores, the echoes ring,
A clam named Carl wants to sing.
"Don't be shy!" the dolphins cheer,
While gulls squawk, another round of beer!

With a splash and a flip, they dive in,
Fish giggling at their watery spin.
"Join our circus!" a crab does shout,
As starfish cheer and the sea snails pout.

Beneath the waves, the mirth does swell,
As sea creatures weave their tale to tell.
"Life's a party!" they chant with glee,
To the echoes of joy, come dance with me!

Dance of Shadows on the Water

While shadows prance on the moonlit beams,
The fish are twirling in aquatic dreams.
Octopuses twist in a frothy jive,
As the water winks, feeling alive!

With every splash, a laugh takes flight,
Merfolk join in, what a silly sight!
"I can do the worm!" a clam does boast,
As angry lobsters dance their toast.

The sea cucumber's got some moves,
With wobbling steps, it surely grooves.
Seahorses sway, they form a train,
While weathered buoys cheer with veiled disdain.

Under the stars, a shimm'ring bash,
As ripples chuckle, loud and brash.
With laughter shared, they sway along,
In the shallow waters, they sing their song!

Light Kisses the Coral Embrace

Coral reefs wear the night like a crown,
With color and laughter, they won't drown.
A clam's got jokes, his humor's bright,
As the sea fans sway in sheer delight.

The turtles spin, in graceful flight,
Sharing secrets with fish so bright.
They gossip 'bout the sunken ship,
Where treasure waits, but first a sip!

A conch shell blows, it's time to rave,
With all the waves, they dance and wave.
"Join the fun!" cries the shrimp with glee,
In the bubble dance, let's all be free!

As light kisses waves, a party starts,
With ticklish barnacles, and merry hearts.
They celebrate life, both big and small,
In the coral embrace, there's room for all!

Waves of Enchantment and Serenity

The sea is a joker, a wave in disguise,
It tickles your toes and plays with your sighs.
Fish wear top hats, and crabs tap dance,
The ocean's a party—a slippery chance.

Seagulls wear shades, squawking with glee,
As dolphins do flips, just to amuse thee.
A treasure chest filled with jelly-filled treats,
Who knew that soft sand could taste so sweet?

The moon beams a smile, a twinkle so bright,
As starfish gossip about life at night.
Clams sing their songs, a horrible tune,
But it's all in good fun under the moon.

The tides do a jig, the shore does a spin,
Where the silly seaweed invites you to grin.
Splashing and laughing till the break of dawn,
In this whimsical place, we dance till we're drawn.

Ebbing Emotions under the Night Sky

The waves whisper secrets of lost fishy dreams,
While seals share deep thoughts through bubbled schemes.
The ocean's a therapist, quite out of sight,
With starfish advising, 'Just chill for tonight.'

Crabs click their claws to a comical beat,
As mermaids drop pearls while they dance on their feet.
The tide pools gossip about tides of love,
While jellyfish float like balloons from above.

With glimmers of laughter beneath twinkling stars,
The pufferfish jokes, leaving no room for scars.
Ebbing emotions with a wink from the tide,
In silliness found, we'll take it in stride.

As seaweed chuckles, we're drawn to the shore,
This night brings us joy, who could want more?
With waves that embrace us, we laugh out loud,
In the harbor of happiness, we're part of the crowd.

Sirens' Songs in the Glistening Dark

Sirens are singing their enchanting tunes,
Baiting lost sailors with sweet, silly boons.
Their melodies bubble, a whimsical cheer,
We can't take them serious, they sound like a deer.

With fishy fables and tales of the sea,
They lure sailors in with a giggle and glee.
But watch out, dear sailor, don't take the bait,
For this merry mishap could seal your fate.

Bubbles of laughter rise high from below,
As octopuses juggle in a bright ocean show.
Their eight arms are waving, a party so grand,
With glittering scales all across the sand.

In the glow of the moon, the sirens will frown,
When sailors just giggle and dance all around.
For who needs their melodies when laughter's the key,
In the glistening dark, we choose to be free.

Journey of the Night-Bound Sailor

A sailor sets sail with a wink and a grin,
His compass is broken, flapping like skin.
He charts silly waves on a map made of cheese,
This journey's absurd, but it aims to please.

The stars are his guide, giving him cheer,
While sea turtles giggle, 'What brings you here?'
He sings with the whales, a laughable tune,
As gulls play cards in the light of the moon.

His ship made of paper faces the tide,
With jellyfish helping, his spirit won't hide.
Through swells that lead nowhere, he dances, he sways,
In the antics of night, he finds new ways.

With horizons of dreams and a barrel of fun,
He sails through the night till the rising sun.
In the heart of the sea, he'll always remain,
A sailor of laughter, his joy is the gain.

Silhouettes Danced by the Celestial Glow

In the soft glow where shadows prance,
Crabs in tuxedos join the dance.
A seagull squawks a cheeky tune,
As starfish sway beneath the moon.

The jellyfish flaunt, all in a row,
In their night club, putting on a show.
Fish twirl round in glittery caps,
While dolphins giggle, making maps.

Shells all clink like glasses raised,
To a party night, all amazed.
The tide brings snacks, a feast so grand,
As octopuses lead a conga band.

So if you stroll along the shore,
Beware of sea critters wanting more.
Laughter bubbles with waves so bright,
Join the fun beneath the night!

Mysteries of the Shores at Midnight

Beneath the sky, a riddle stirs,
Where crabs wear hats and greet you purrs.
Seashells gossip, exchanging tales,
Of fishy dates and windy gales.

A sandpiper hops with a swagger bold,
Claiming it's part of a band from old.
The tide swoops in with a playful grin,
Like a friend who loves to dive right in.

Look! A mermaid caught in a net,
Trying to tango, not quite set.
Nearby, a clam clams up in fright,
As dolphins plan a late-night flight.

Mysteries dance in waves so spry,
With bright-eyed critters, oh my, oh my!
Set your clocks, it's party time,
Where laughter ties like a perfect rhyme.

Shadows of Light on Ocean's Palette

Painted skies hold whispers of fun,
As seagulls nap in the glowing sun.
The ocean's canvas, a silly sight,
Fish asking turtles to join their flight.

Crabs wear shades, all chill and fly,
While mermaids tease the waves nearby.
Shadows quirk like a funny haiku,
Riding ripples like a breezy crew.

Nautical nonsense leads the way,
As starfish spin in a waltz ballet.
Under the glow, the critters play,
In nature's art, they twist and sway.

So raise a fin, a claw, a vibe,
For underwater jests, it's quite a tribe!
Paint your night with laughter and cheer,
For joy is brightest in oceans here!

Nighttime Whispers Beneath the Stars

In the cool night, secrets unfold,
Where sea turtles share tales of old.
With whispers soft as a wave's gentle kiss,
Fishes plot mischief, quite hard to miss.

A starfish snickers at passing boats,
While seashells argue over who botes.
The lighthouse blinks with a cheeky grin,
Yet even the crabs feel the fun begin.

Moonbeams tickle the ocean's face,
As octopuses join in the race.
Playful poppers, with bubbles so bright,
Sparkling laughter in the heart of night.

So listen closely, the sea it speaks,
Of quirky lives and playful peaks.
Join the dance, let the tides convey,
Under this sky, laughter holds sway!

Dance of the Clouded Reflections

The seashells giggle on the sand,
While starfish dance, oh isn't it grand?
A crab doing the cha-cha with style,
Seagulls swoop in, but they're not worthwhile.

The octopus juggles with eight floppy limbs,
Turtles in top hats, oh what a whim!
They sip on lemonade, quite the delight,
Underneath stars in the fading light.

The jellyfish waltz with a jelly-like grace,
Shuffling around in a watery space.
Anemones whisper secrets with glee,
As the tide rolls in, they throw a grand spree.

Oh, the beach is alive with laughter and cheer,
With silly sea friends who all gather near.
So let's join the frolic, come one, come all,
In this whimsical dance, we'll have a ball!

Midnight Secrets of Forgotten Shores

On the sand, where shadows play tricks,
Crabs tell tales of their beachside kicks,
With whispers of wind and salt in the air,
Once-upon-a-time fish, they lounge without care.

The moon makes a face, all pucker and pout,
While seaweed giggles, oh what's that about?
A fish in a tux is making a toast,
To mermaids who party and dance like a ghost.

Seashells are gossiping, what nonsense they weave,
"Have you seen that dolphin? He's hard to believe!"
The waves roll in, making laughter abound,
As starfish flip-flop, they're lost but not found.

Oh, the beaches are filled with bright silly sights,
As clowns in the tides have their own late-night bites.
A treasure of joy from the depths of the blue,
Midnight secrets shared, just for me and you!

Twilit Reflections in a Salted Pool

In puddles of salt, the fish take a dive,
While upside-down berries roll in laughter's hive.
Flappy-tailed guppies in hats made of leaves,
Raise a ruckus as twilight softly weaves.

Crabs wearing glasses argue over the snack,
While a clam on the side gives a friendly whack.
"Come share our secrets!" the seaweed begs low,
In a bubbling pool where the wild stories flow.

The sun yawns and stretches, it's time to unwind,
As otters play leapfrog, oh aren't they quite blind?
They splash and they giggle, such fun in the glow,
In salty reflections where chaos can grow.

So join in the fray, there's silliness here,
With friends from the depths that we hold so dear.
With frisbees of foam and a pop from the tide,
Twilit laughter awaits, let your worries subside!

Harmonies of the Deep Blue Night

A symphony rises from the waves with a crash,
With dolphins composing a marvelous mash.
Octopuses strum on their coral guitars,
While fish form a choir, under gaze of the stars.

The shrimp tap their feet, quite skilled at the beat,
With mackerel dancing, their twirls quite sweet.
But wait! There's a seal with a nose quite large,
Leading the tune, proclaiming, "I'm in charge!"

The crabs join in, with their claws making sound,
As sea urchins hum, spreading joy all around.
A whale belts a note that could shatter the night,
And the other sea creatures all cheer in delight.

So gather your friends beneath twinkling lights,
To witness their antics, full of giggles and sights.
In harmonies deep, let the laughter ignite,
For fun in the ocean is pure and just right!

Glimmering Tales from the Shoreline

On a beach where crabs hold court,
They wear tiny crowns, of course!
Waves come crashing, what a noise,
Seagulls squawk like silly boys.

A fish in glasses, quite the sight,
Said, "I'm ready for a fishing flight!"
A single wave knocked him down.
And he rolled back, lost his crown!

Shells tell stories, quite absurd,
Whisper secrets, strange and blurred.
A starfish says, "Let's dance tonight!"
But crabs just scuttle, yikes, what fright!

The tide pulls in, the tide pulls out,
And all the seaweed starts to pout.
"Why can't we join the crab parade?"
A clam replied, "We're just too laid!"

Veils of Mist and Starlit Dreams

When the moon gets a little shy,
Stars giggle as they float on by.
Fish wear hats, they're dressed to thrill,
Singing tunes with flippered skill.

A dolphin jokes, "What's with the tide?"
"Maybe it's on an underwater ride!"
All the sandcastles start to sway,
As waves crash in, they say, "Oh yay!"

Crabs line up for a dance-off show,
While the octopus steals the glow.
Bubbles rise like tiny balloons,
While jellyfish hum silly tunes.

The starry skies start to twirl,
A comet whirls, gives a swirl.
But then it gets stuck in the tide,
And the fish laugh, "What a wild ride!"

Cradled by the Night's Caress

Underneath a lantern fish,
A squid makes quite a funny wish.
"I'd like to join a human feast!"
But then he realized, he'd be the least!

Seashells spin tales of the past,
With echoes of laughter that last.
A crab declares, "I'm king tonight!"
Then loses his throne in a laugh-out-loud fight.

Anemones giggle, waving arms,
While her friends tease her about her charms.
"Let's throw a party, make it grand!"
But the jellyfish all just blanched!

A turtle arrives on a skateboard,
"Am I cool or just a gourd?"
He wobbled and tumbled in a spin,
"Next time, I'll bring my fins!"

Tides of Reflection and Reverie

A ship made of pretzels floats by,
While snacks wave hello, oh my!
The captain's a seagull with flair,
"We're off to find tasty fish fare!"

Reflections dance on the surface bright,
Where mermaids make wishes at night.
But one's stuck trying to tie a bow,
While her friends giggle at the show!

A sea otter floats with a grin,
Juggling fish while trying to swim.
"Oh, look at me!" he starts to gleam,
But the fish jump up like part of a dream!

The tides keep pulling, a wild swirl,
As clams form a conga line whirl.
With every wave, a new fun spree,
As the ocean laughs, wild and free!

Shadows Cast by Lunar Dreams

A crab in a suit, dancing with flair,
Made everyone laugh, with his wobbly air.
Stars chuckled softly, in the sky so bright,
While fish wore top hats, what a silly sight!

The seaweed swayed, throwing a grand ball,
A clam played the piano, with grace, not at all.
Dolphins performed, in their best tuxedos,
Splashing and laughing, oh, how the time goes!

Seagulls cheered loudly, such comic relief,
As jellyfish jived, beyond all belief.
The night wore a grin, as humor took flight,
With laughter and joy, in the soft silver light.

So if you glance down, at the beach's dark sand,
You'll see all the fun, that's so grandly planned.
These shadows of dreams, cast by gleeful beams,
Will linger forever, in your playful dreams.

The Sea's Serenade at Twilight

A fish in a tux, with a bowtie so neat,
Sang to the waves, with a tune full of beat.
Octopuses clapped, with their big squishy hands,
While turtles tapped toes, on the soft golden sands.

Seagulls were swooping, with snacks on their mind,
Trading old stories, each one more unkind.
The crabs shared tall tales, with a wink in their eye,
As the stars winked back, in the darkening sky.

The sea foam giggled, in a frothy white dress,
Tickling the shells, in a bubbly caress.
Bubbles floated up, carrying whispers of cheer,
Making all sea creatures feel light as a sphere.

With laughter and song, the blue waters glowed,
As the sea's serenade, joyfully flowed.
So come heed the call, of the night's silly charms,
Where the salt in the air, is laughter in arms.

Crystalline Tears of the Night

The moonlight wept, with pearls made of glow,
As fish true comedians stole all the show.
They juggled sea stars, and laughed till it hurt,
While snails chose to race, then got lost in the dirt.

A whale told a joke, about a tall sinking ship,
Which sent all the dolphins into a mad flip.
Their laughter echoed, like waves on the shore,
A symphony grand, who could ask for more?

The jellybeans jived, with bounce in their step,
While clam friends snickered, in a clammy inept.
Bubbles burst laughing, floating up to the sky,
Where stars twinkled brightly, not a one was shy.

Tears of joy sparkled, like diamond-studded light,
Painting the ocean in colors so bright.
Each drop a giggle, each wave a new cheer,
Embracing the humor, that fills the night air.

Echoes of the Distant Horizon

On the beach it was strange, with the tide's funny flow,
As otters wore shades, basking high and low.
They traded old jokes, with a wink and a grin,
While starfish played chess, let the games begin!

The moon cast a laugh, which rippled the sea,
As clumsy sea urchins slipped off with glee.
Mermaids spun tales, of fish that could dance,
And seagulls flew high, hoping for a chance.

The horizon echoed, with whimsical sounds,
As critters all gathered, on the playful grounds.
With shells as their drums, they beat out a tune,
That stirred up the night, 'neath the light of the moon.

So join in the fun, let your worries take flight,
For life's just a game, in the soft, silly night.
With echoes of laughter, and joy so profound,
The ocean's sweet humor, is always around.

Silver Snatches of the Sea's Heart

Waves whisper secrets, dressed in foam,
Crabs do a cha-cha, claiming their home.
Fish wearing sunglasses swim by with flair,
Octopuses giggle, waving tentacle hair.

Seagulls take selfies, they strike silly poses,
While clams flip-flop in brightly colored clothes.
Starfish at parties, they shine and they sway,
Jellyfish float gently, in their own ballet.

Sandcastles tumble, the tide takes its shot,
The seashells all cheer, "Was that a good plot?"
Mermaids tell tales, with a wink and a grin,
Scooping up laughter, let the fun begin!

So here by the shore, there's always a show,
Where giggles and bubbles consistently flow.
In the playful embrace of the moon's silver light,
The ocean keeps smiling, and everything's bright.

The Midnight Dance of Glimmering Sands

Sandy toes tap to the tide's gentle beat,
Crabs in tuxedos, what a classy feat!
Shells form a band, with a soft, sneaky swipe,
And a dolphin DJ spins the night with hype.

The stars overhead are a glittery stage,
While fish flip-flop, escaping a cage.
Eels do the twist, on the shore they prance,
Punchlines and punch-outs in a splashing dance.

Seagulls mount mics, and they croon with delight,
As the breeze tells a joke, keeping it light.
Mermaids with glitter perform in a splash,
While seaweed sways, like a soft, gentle stash.

Laughter rings clear as the moon takes a bow,
With every wave crash, they're saying, "Wow!"
In this whimsical realm, night wears a grin,
Let's party till dawn, let the fun times begin!

Reflected Dreams in the Ocean's Cradle

Starfish swim by wearing shades of pale pink,
While sea cucumbers giggle without a blink.
The moon reflects secrets on water's smooth face,
Crabs crack jokes in an undersea race.

Glimmering silvers twinkle in rhythm divine,
A dance of the waves, it's a sight so fine.
Lobsters in puns, making jokes without fear,
As turtles spin tales, lending fins to cheer.

Seashells hold whispers of laughter and fun,
While breezes come calling, a soft, gentle run.
The ocean holds dreams in its salty embrace,
As fish swap tall stories, embracing the space.

Under waves pulsing, laughter will bloom,
With a splash and a dash, there's always more room.
And as night unfolds with its rhythmic soft hum,
In this cradle of dreams, there's magic and fun!

Choreography of the Night Sea

In the goofy glow of a watery disco,
Seashells do the hustle, putting on a show.
The currents create beats, a whirl from the blue,
As seaweed sways freely, just like a crew.

The moonbeams flicker like spotlights on high,
While fish do the backstroke, oh my, oh my!
Dolphins do flips, in a splash of bright cheer,
And a clam snickers softly, "This party's my beer."

Crabs take a turn, shaking legs in delight,
While seagulls provide soaring jokes in flight.
A turtle twirls slow, with grace in each motion,
The jellyfish bounce to the joyful commotion.

As the laughter bubbles and the night drifts along,
The sea joins the dance, and it all feels so strong.
With a glee that's contagious, they dance 'til it's done,
In this quirky ocean, the night's just begun!

Whispers of the Ocean Night

The crabs hold a party, all dancing on sand,
With seaweed as streamers, it's quite unplanned.
They gossip of fish, and the octopus' bow,
While seagulls keep laughing, just don't ask how.

The starfish tell stories of their grand tours,
Of hitchhiking dolphins and beach bum cures.
With pearls in their fists, they toast to the tide,
While the jellyfish giggle, they've nothing to hide.

A clam tries to sing in a slightly flat key,
The shrimp start to chuckle, oh what a spree!
A wave gives a nudge, it all goes astray,
As everyone tumbles, then joins in the play.

As moonlight does shimmer on water so bright,
Each creature erupts into joy for the night.
With laughter and splashes, they dance to their tune,
Under the sparkle of the whimsical moon.

Secrets Beneath the Silver Waves

A fish with a top hat swims by exclaiming,
"Why don't we invite the sharks? They're just so charming!"
The octopus winks, saying, "They swim up for laughs,
With whiskers like humor, let's calculate gaffs!"

The sea turtles roll with a leisurely grace,
They gossip and giggle, then lose the race.
The crabs in a corner lay bets with delight,
While a dolphin bets double—what a fierce night!

An eel tells a tale of the biggest sea quest,
Of treasure so shiny, but mostly just jest.
The clams all are snickering, trying to blink,
At the flatfish who fakes it—oh, can you think?

As laughter erupts from the deep azure sea,
They toast with a splash, "Here's to silly glee!"
With ripples of joy spinning round and around,
These secrets are treasures forever unbound.

Lullabies of the Celestial Sea

The jellyfish jive to a tune of the night,
While singing starfish take their turn to ignite.
With bubbles as bass and a seashell for drums,
The laughter erupts, oh, the silliness hums!

A crab in a tux claims he knows how to croon,
But his voice sounds quite funny—like a confused balloon.
The sardines are swaying, all packed in a row,
As the blennies are blushing, a bashful show!

With turtles that twirl and a sea cucumber's dance,
They whirl through the waves in a lively romance.
The sea snakes all chuckle, their wiggling a sight,
As the seashells clap shells, what a glorious night!

So once more the moon smiles on the vibrant spree,
While crabs keep the beat, and the fish sing with glee.
These lullabies echo through every bright wave,
In the heart of the ocean, from silly to brave.

Dreams Adrift in Lunar Gleam

A narwhal's on roller skates, what a wild ride,
He spins and he twirls, with such fishy pride.
The sea urchins cheer, a fuzzy parade,
While the barnacles beep, oh the fun that they've made!

A whale tells a joke, though it sputters and splashes,
Yet the punchline arrives amid giggles and crashes.
The dolphins explode in a fit of delight,
With echoes of laughter brightening the night.

With a clam on a trumpet and lobsters that sing,
They serenade all, it's a comical fling.
The squids throw confetti of ink in the air,
As the bottom feeders wiggle without a care!

The tide rolls along, with a wink and a sway,
As everyone joins in the merry cabaret.
In the glow of the night, they all laugh and gleam,
In this world of the waves, where fun's the main theme.

Enigma of the Glimmering Waves

The fish wore hats with glee,
Dancing jigs by the sea.
Crabs joined in with a cheer,
Sipping soda, oh so clear.

Seashells giggled as they spun,
Claiming shells, oh what fun!
Starfish flipped, they took a bow,
In this dance, who knows how?

Seagulls laughed, their beaks a-tease,
Chasing waves with the greatest ease.
Jellyfish in their jelly shoes,
Swaying slowly, singing blues.

But the tide had a trick or two,
Waves would splash and say boo!
That made everyone run away,
Back to the shore, oh what a play!

Ocean's Heartbeat Beneath the Stars

A dolphin wore a funky tie,
Sailed through waves with a cheerful sigh.
Octopuses played the saxophone,
Filling the night with a jazzy tone.

Starfish joined a talent show,
In the spotlight, stealing the glow.
With one big slap, they sang out loud,
Making the whole ocean proud.

A whale slid in, doing the twist,
Claiming the crown that none could resist.
Clownfish chuckled, pulling pranks,
Swapping hats in a body of tanks.

As the tide giggled with delight,
The stars blinked back with a wink so bright.
Under the waves, a party grew,
Laughter echoed, all night through!

The Dark Canvas of Celestial Spells

Seahorses painted in polka dots,
Swam in patterns, tying knots.
Mermaids played with bubbles of air,
Fashioning hats with a breezy flair.

Glowworms danced in the midnight sea,
Crafting light with joyful decrees.
Anemones joined the swirling spree,
Making waves with laughter, oh so free.

Pirate fish, with their eyepatch bold,
Told tales of treasures and legends old.
While snails slid by in a slow parade,
Casting rhymes in the ocean's shade.

Waves wrapped secrets in silvery coils,
Bubbling whispers, like playful foils.
With laughter bright in the depth's embrace,
The ocean's canvas held a quirky grace!

Murmurs of the Moonlit Depths

The clams held a poetry slam,
Reciting verses with a joyful jam.
Worms on stage did a silly jig,
Making the crowd laugh and dig.

Shy squids painted with colorful flare,
Donned sequined costumes, quite rare.
Their ink was spellbound, pink and blue,
Splashing funny shapes as the ocean flew.

Crabs in tuxedos tiptoed around,
Hoping for laughter that would resound.
Seashells whispered gossip like mad,
"Did you hear what the starfish had?"

As the dance floor swayed to and fro,
The moon smirked down, putting on a show.
With bubbles tickling fins in the night,
All of ocean's laughter, a pure delight!

Secrets Unraveled by the Moon's Glow

Bubbles rise and secrets dive,
When fish gossip, they come alive.
Lobsters dance with great delight,
As crabs laugh, oh what a sight!

A starfish winks, what a charade,
While seagulls squawk, they serenade.
With shrimp in hats, a party's near.
This underwater prom we cheer!

The jellyfish glide in silly spins,
While barnacles sport their party fins.
The seaweed sways, a luscious green,
In this wacky world, we're all a team!

When tides retreat, the laughs will swell,
For every tide has tales to tell.
As bubbles burst in merry glee,
Secrets float, come dance with me!

The Dreamer's Lament on Sea's Edge

A mermaid yawns and flips her hair,
Her fishy friends just giggle and stare.
With dreams of beach balls oh so round,
She drifts on waves, her laugh a sound!

The gulls chase dreams of sandwich treats,
While crabs compete in beach-front feats.
With flip-flops on, I trip and fall,
And hear a starfish softly call.

"Oh dear," I sigh, "what a great plan!"
The octopus waves, like a great fan.
With dreams of dancing on the shore,
The sand tickles, oh, I want more!

As wild waves crash with joyful force,
I tip my hat, the sea's my horse.
In dreams, oh dreams, we laugh and play,
At the sea's edge, it's a funny day!

Whispers of the Silver Waves

The waves whisper secrets in shifts and sways,
Where dolphins tell jokes in playful ways.
A clam snickers at the passing tide,
While octopuses grin with pearls inside.

The moon giggles down with a silvery sheen,
As fish form a band, brilliant and keen.
With seaweed garlands upon their heads,
They dance in circles, just like they said.

A starfish plays drums; oh, what a score!
The conchs play trumpets, we all shout for more!
With every wave, laughter and cheer,
These oceanic jesters make joy clear.

So come take a dip in this jolly sea,
Where waves are the punchlines, wild and free.
When night falls soft with its giggles and sighs,
The silver waves shine with sparkle and highs!

Night's Embrace on Salty Shores

With salty air, the night finds fun,
As waves crash down, we all just run.
Giggling shells hide treasures bright,
While crabs scuttle left in sheer delight.

A sea turtle yawns, "What a long day!"
She wears a sunhat, come join the fray.
With beach balls bouncing through the sand,
The stars chuckle down, how cleverly planned!

The sandcastle kingdom, oh what a sight,
Getting washed away in the sheer moonlight.
"Let's rebuild!" the children all cheer,
As laughter echoes far and near.

So here we dance on silver shores,
In the moon's embrace, mischief restores.
With waves as our music, let's make it grand,
As night falls softly on this salty land!

Luminous Pathways of Liquid Light

The jellyfish dance in a wobbly trance,
As fish wear their brightest pants.
Crabs do the cha-cha on the sand,
While seagulls squawk their marching band.

The waves play tag with a zippy splash,
Seashells giggle, they're quite brash.
Starfish twirl with a clumsy flair,
As the ocean laughs and flips its hair.

The tide rolls in with a playful shove,
Shells rattle like they're in love.
A dolphin dives in a silly spree,
Practicing moves for a fishy jamboree.

Crabs throw a party in the surf's cool foam,
Jokingly calling the ocean their home.
With every splash, the fun takes flight,
Dancing merrily through the night.

Songs of the Siren's Cove

In the cove where the fishes hum tunes,
Mermaids wear hats made of loony balloons.
Unicorns prance on the waves' gentle crest,
Shouting, "We've come for a jellybean quest!"

Octopuses strum on a seaweed guitar,
Their sea-shanties reach as near as a star.
The sea urchins join in, a spiky delight,
As bubbles burst with giggles in flight.

Sea turtles bob in a conga line,
With sunglasses on, they think they're divine.
A clam claps along with a rhythmic snap,
The tides sway to this funny mishap.

The chorus of crabs leads the fun parade,
Throwing bubbles as confetti is made.
Every wave is a giggle, a song,
Singing joyfully right along.

Ocean Breath Beneath Starry Skies

The sea snickers as it pulls away,
Making all the driftwood sway.
Sandcastles giggle, with moats that splash,
As waves march in with a water ballet clash.

Fish with hats swim in a quirky race,
Giggling as they drink from a shell's embrace.
Starfish play games of hide and seek,
Tickling the barnacles, not a bit meek.

The moon winks down with a silver grin,
As frogs join in with a croaky din.
A dolphin cracks jokes with a flip so spry,
Making the crabs chuckle, oh my, oh my!

Each ripple bubbles with laughter anew,
In the whispers of wind, the giggles ensue.
What fun swims in this ocean's glide,
With mirthful magic on every tide.

Caresses of the Night Breeze

The night breeze tickles the ocean's face,
As stars giggle in a twinkly race.
The waves whisper secrets to the sand,
While sea cucumbers form a funny band.

Seagulls are gossiping, flying high,
With tales of fish who dream to fly.
Crabs trade jokes on a sandy path,
Rolling in laughter at their own math.

A turtle strolls with a haughty flair,
Though slowly, as if it hasn't a care.
Starfish compete for the best hat crown,
With every splash, they tumble down.

As night unfolds its shimmering veil,
The ocean hums a whimsical tale.
A place where laughter's always in breeze,
And jokestars twinkle in easy tease.

Starlit Currents and Whispering Sands

The waves giggle and play,
As crabs dance on the shore,
Seagulls squawk all day,
Dreaming of snacks galore.

Sandcastles loom tall and bright,
With moats filled with giggles,
Shells in a feathery fright,
At the tickling of the wiggles.

Fishermen's boats sway and sway,
Telling tall tales of catches,
While starfish join in the fray,
Wearing fancy, seaweed patches.

Even the tide can't resist,
The charm of a good fish joke,
With splashes that twist and twist,
And laughter that never chokes.

Dreaming Beneath the Night's Veil

The moon sneezed, the stars replied,
What an odd little tune!
Fish in tuxedos, taking a ride,
Through a world of silver spoon.

Jellyfish with light-up hats,
They wiggle and flop in style,
While dolphins chat about cool stats,
And how to surf a while.

A crab played a shiny sax,
And made the clams tap dance,
With rhythm that never lacks,
They swayed in a sea romance.

Laughter echoed through the night,
As seaweed tossed and twirled,
Fish, crabs, and shells in delight,
Celebrating the ocean's world.

Luminescent Ripples in the Dark

The waves shimmer like broad smiles,
As octopuses prance about,
Starfish tell their sea-floor files,
While eels wiggle with a shout.

Seashells click and clack, a band,
As every crab claps its claws,
Whales hum their tunes so grand,
Rehearsing for the crowd's applause.

Glowworms float like little boats,
With jellyfish twirling by,
Anemones share funny quotes,
While neighbors wave hi and bye.

The tide pulls back for a grin,
As night wraps the sea in glee,
With laughter bubbling within,
A party for all to see.

The Call of the Nighttime Sea

The call of the waves is loud,
A seal cracks jokes on the rocks,
Squid make up a clever crowd,
With antics that shock the flocks.

Pelicans dive with a splash,
Stealing snacks from the shore,
While sand dollars juggle and dash,
In a comedy show encore.

The tide tickles toes all around,
As crabs scamper in a race,
With saltwater laughter unbound,
And starfish winking in place.

When the night whispers a tune,
The ocean hums a song,
Under this enchanting moon,
It feels like joy lasts long.

The Pull of Darkness and Light

In a world of black and white,
Where shadows dance with delight,
The crab wears shades, feeling sly,
While the fish just giggles by.

Whispers from the depths arise,
As clams reveal their silly lies,
The seaweed does the twist and shout,
While starfish cheer and wave about.

A jellyfish has an electric glow,
Doing the cha-cha, putting on a show,
The moon, it watches with a wink,
As fish jump high, but rarely sink.

With bubbles bursting in delight,
And shrimps that leap into the night,
The ocean's giggles fill the air,
As creatures dance without a care.

Twilight's Embrace on the Briny Deep

As sun dips down, the laughter flows,
A dolphin giggles, a fishy nose grows,
With every splash, the sea's alive,
As sea turtles roll and high-fives thrive.

Octopus dons a polka dot tie,
While seahorses giggle and glide by,
The barnacles tell corny jokes,
As pufferfish puff, entertaining folks.

With each wave crashing, the fun's a blast,
A sea cucumber slow dances at last,
The light fades softly, but cheer won't flee,
As jellybeans drift, wild and free.

The tide tickles toes as it creeps,
While crabs tell stories that nobody keeps,
The night whispers secrets without a peep,
In their twilight embrace, the ocean leaps.

Moonbeams and Salty Breezes

With moonbeams shining on the waves,
The fish get frolicsome in their caves,
A narwhal sports a funky hat,
While anemones dance in spat!

The sea foam giggles as it rolls,
Tickling the fins of fishy souls,
The night air filled with salty cheer,
As mermaids sing, they've nothing to fear.

Giant squids play peek-a-boo,
While whales hold contests what can they do,
Bubbles burst, laughter-filled,
In this watery realm, joy is spilled.

As jellyfish twirl in their moonlit attire,
The ocean floor's their dance empire,
From crabs to clams, a laugh parade,
In nature's ball, they all get laid.

An Ode to the Ocean's Secrets

In the deep where secrets sway,
Clams gossip in a curious way,
With whispers carried by the tide,
The silly tales the fishes hide.

A turtle thinks he's quite the star,
As seaweed floats in a silly car,
The crabs are plotting their next big prank,
On creatures swimming in the prankster bank.

Bubbles rise with giggles high,
As a clownfish makes a comical pie,
The waters echo with roofs of glee,
As they stitch their tales beneath the sea.

With every wave, a joke is cast,
From dolphins surfing, oh so fast,
In the ocean's heart, laughter finds,
Hidden treasures leave us in binds.

Salty Kisses in a Luminous Night

The fish are dancing, what a sight,
They wriggle and giggle in pure delight.
Crabs in tuxedos, they waddle so bright,
While seaweed sways in the silvery light.

Jellyfish giggle with gloopy grace,
Playing tag with shells in a watery race.
A dolphin with jokes, what a goofy face,
As we all share in this splashy embrace.

Starfish gossip, what silly chat,
"Did you see that seal in a top hat?"
A lobster in shades looks fancy and fat,
While octopuses spin in a raucous spat.

So raise your glass to this beachy spree,
With salty kisses, so wild and free.
The moon shines down, can't you see?
It's a night of laughter, just you and me!

The Melodic Embrace of the Abyss

Down in the depths where the mermaids play,
With shells for drums, they dance all day.
A bass guitar strums, the fish sway,
While a turtle raps in his own funny way.

"We'll start a band!" shouts a brave little squid,
As sea cucumbers cheer, they know he's amid.
Even the clams join in with a lid,
Jellyfish swirl while the beats are rid.

An octopus croons in a silky voice,
"Join the party, you've got no choice!"
With bubbles as mics, we're all in rejoice,
For in this sea jam, there's no need for poise.

So let's groove in the hall of coral bright,
Where laughter echoes through the deep of night.
Every fin and every tail feels right,
In this ocean boogie, we are all light!

Ebbing Dreams Beneath Celestial Canopies

The tide rolls in with a cheeky grin,
As waves sprinkle dreams on the ocean kin.
Starfish gossip about a fish's win,
While a seahorse prances, wearing a pin.

A crab throws a party, oh what a scene,
With shrimp as the DJ, and it's quite the routine.
Mollusks are dancing, looking so keen,
While clams wave their shells, keep it all clean.

"Don't forget snacks!" cries a hungry old eel,
As plankton stream in, ready to steal.
The laughter and joy, the perfect ideal,
In a moonlit glow, it's a tasty meal.

So let's dance till dawn, till our fins ache,
In the salty embrace, let's make a mistake.
With ebbing dreams and a wave of the brake,
We'll giggle and wiggle, for laughter's our stake!

Moonlit Mystique of the Ocean Floor

The floor is a dance floor, watch out now,
With crabs doing the cha-cha, take a bow.
Anemones sway, don't know how,
Clams join in, they're part of the wow!

"Is that a goldfish in a top hat?"
"Why yes, and he's quite the aristocrat!"
A dolphin serves drinks, oh imagine that,
While all of us sway in our sea critter spat.

A seagull joins late, he's not even shy,
He swoops to the beat with a jubilant cry.
Starfish are spinning as if to comply,
With a wink and a nod, oh me, oh my!

With laughter and bubbles, we twirl and glide,
In this ocean spectacle, joy is our guide.
The moonlight shines bright, an enchanting tide,
As we dance and rejoice, let worries subside!

www.ingramcontent.com/pod-product-compliance
Lightning Source LLC
Chambersburg PA
CBHW062109280426
43661CB00086B/379